The Healing of a

The Healing
of a Broken World

(tikkum olam)

DAVID JAFFIN

to the memory of Viktor E. Frankl

First published in the United Kingdom in 2017 by
Shearsman Books
50 Westons Hill Drive
Emersons Green
Bristol BS16 7DF

Shearsman Books Ltd Registered Office
30–31 St. James Place, Mangotsfield, Bristol BS16 9JB
(this address not for correspondence)

www.shearsman.com

ISBN 978-1-84861-405-5

Distributed for Shearsman Books in the U. S. A.
by Small Press Distribution, 1341 Seventh Avenue, Berkeley, CA 94710
E-Mail orders@spdbooks.org
www.spdbooks.org

Production, composition, & cover design: Edition Wortschatz, a service of
Neufeld Verlag, Cuxhaven/Germany
E-Mail info@edition-wortschatz.de, www.edition-wortschatz.de

Title photograph:
Hannelore Bäumler, München

Printed in Germany

Contents

13

14

15

With continuing thanks
to Marina Moisel
for the preparation
of this manuscript

and to Hanni Bäumler
for her well-placed photograph

For me good poetry has always meant a unity between sound, sense, image and idea – a prevading mood-tonality. There must never be a word too many – poetry as the art of compression, "saying the most by using the least". The main adversary is cliché – using words the way they've been usually used. Poetry should take-on a cleansing function, letting words and the context-of-words shine again as newly-minted coins. Every poet tends to have his own clichés, his own oft half-routine ways of expression. These must be discovered and eliminated. Such "contaminated" poems are those ca. a quarter-of-the-whole which will be discarded.

My poetry actually "began" through a reading Wallace Stevens gave at the YMHA in New York in the early 1950s – the best of these poems such as *13 Ways of Looking at a Blackbird, The Idea of Order at Key West, 2 Letters* (in *Poems Posthumous*), *Peter Quince at the Clavier, The Snowman* ... were republished in the excellent obituary on Stevens which appeared in *Time Magazine*. I sent Stevens some of my earliest poems and he responded with words I'll never forget: "You must be your own hardest critic." I've always taken those words to heart. Aside from these particular poems of Stevens the central influence on my poetry has continued to remain those great adagios of Joseph Haydn, where space, measure, and sound derive a lasting unity-of-sense.

My earliest books are generally of a quality which continues to satisfy my own aesthetic sense, they were very deliminated in theme. After years of devoting myself to another calling, that of preaching and writing about Jesus the Jew (via the Old Testament) in post-Auschwitz Germany, poetry suddenly and unexpectedly overcame me on a train to Dortmund in 1989. Ever since then, and especially in the 21st century, I've become perhaps the most prolific of poets, and that in my aging years. Why?

Because of the many-interior-tensions within my very-being and also because of my depth of interest and education in various fields. Those tensions, so explicit in my poetry are between The Christian and The Jew, between being an American and a German, between an active and an interior religious life, between time and timelessness ... I am a very one-sided person, but those fields I've made my-own I've depthed as well as I could: literature, classical music, art, faith and religion, the nature of history, human understanding, love, nature, animal-life, aging and death ...

The poetic process is for me at least two fold: either words come over me and demand a word discovery of their true sense; or ideas on this or that linger in my mind until they can find poetic expression. This is the more difficult for me. The ambiguity of language, open endings, levelled meanings seemingly "contradictory" sense of meaning are characteristic of my intuitively conceived poetry. Each poem should be read at least two or three times, and once, at least, aloud, to discover their intrinsic musicality.

I want to thank my dear wife of 55 years, Rosemarie, my muse, for that love, which is at the essence of my very being.

David Jaffin

P. S. I've often been asked why I break words be-
tween lines. As Lenore, one of my most perceptive
readers said, "You don't really break words between
the lines, but place them within the entire rhythmic
flow of the poem."

As my poems are extremely condensed I don't
want words, especially the longer ones, to be "hang-
ing out", therefore this very musical need for such a
continuing on. Word-break, if one wants to call it
that, means that these words must be put back to-
gether again, almost as if they've become recreated,
newly realized.

His self-re

> newing "diary"
> poetizing
>
> a world of
> kaleidoscop
>
> ic intrica
> cies.

Tracing

> the branched
> curve-length
>
> s of their
> sinuous
>
> ly time-e
> volving
>
> s.

If the dis

> tant pine
> could climb
>
> through
> those inter
>
> ior darkness
> es of its
>
> very-being
> to the height
>
> of nowhere
> s-beyond.

Piano Trio 4

(Beethoven op. 11)

transparent
ly strength

ed to the
depth-control

of only pure
music – noth

ing more than
that!

Schubert

Piano Trio op. 99
s slow move

ment's unknown
world beauti

fied even bey
ond those in

viewed realm
s of time

less perfect
ion.

Fauré's

Piano Trio op. 120
late-romanti

cally involv
ing a suffi

ciently French
taste for o

pen-aired
time-sound

ings.

Transpar

ent touch-e
voking cloud

s weightless
ly time-es

caping.

Spread

ing through
early morn

ing's green
ed soundless

ly shadow
ings.

When the

moon's impend
ing glow mag

netically a
live.

a) When "The

Leopard"
(Lampedusa)

finely blood–
timing

those hidden–
enclosure

s of Sicily'
s centur

ied virgin
lands.

b) A true ser

vant tradit
ioned to

that same
time–holding

cause of his
effetely–sen

sitive mast
er.

c) This time

(1860)

Sicily once-
again invaded

by a "for
eign army"

(though thor
oughly disguis

ed) as if im
pulsing its

own truly
blooded-

serving deceiv
ing source.

d) Does "The

Leopard" im

person (but
yet) another

symbol of a
time-decay

ing past.

Flowed-

dried sap
lessly invok

ing tree–tim
ed fantas

ies.

Kersting'

s reflect
ive solitude

s nightly en
closured.

A garden

paradis
ed with the

scent of a
coloring

expressive
ness.

A bouquet of

flowers left
that room

deeply color
ing its shad

owed awaken
ings.

Where e

ven the wind
s sought a

shadowing
refuge from

their over-
voicing pre

sence.

When for the

middle-aged
"Leopard"

even the
touch of a

young lady'
s perfumed–

fragrance a
wakened a

blood–arous
ing danger–

zone.

Why abandon

ed house
s left an em

ptied impress
ion of untouch

ed–silence
s.

For Rosemarie

Home–coming'
s a return

to where
you've be

come alway
s–there.

When poem

s breathe
their open-

aired still
nesses.

Where Southern

Florida's time-
sunken forest

s echoing-out
but a shall

owed respon
se.

The pond

water-touch
ed its scarce

ly-awaken
ed surfacing

s.

In her late

50s when the
first yellow-

touched leave
s began to

fade her slow
ly self-re

signing im
pression

s.

An inwardly-

forsaken
friendship

at a "chance-
breeze" a

float with
those same

time-flying
color

s.

Low-lying

clouds as if
cushioned

an imposing
softness

of opportune
response.

a) *A summer*

coolness after
the rain's

sensed–down
shadowing

seclusion
s.

b) *When touch*

reveals the
skin-depth

of lost-time
reflection

s.

c) *A twilight*

bird's phrased–
through melodic

intonat
ions.

d) The quiet

time of e
vening's first

indrawn shad
owing still

nesses.

When time

draws its cur
tains down

too tired to
move the poem

beyond its
speechless

presence.

Marin Marais'

darkly inbred
intonation

s remind of
a bear prowl

ing its own
ground-based

foreboding
intention

s.

He awoke

    from a time-en
    compassing

    sleeping-off
    those darkly-

    sensed mood-
    current

    s.

Haydn'

    s slowly in
    creasing symphon

    ic praeludium
    s cosmically

    world-immens
    ing.

Leave's hand-

    made shadow

    ing illusion
    s.

A natural

ly unminding
smile may

imply fresh
ly insinuat

ing reapprais
als.

Holding-back

tightening-
the-reins

to one's im
pulsively

self-assum
ing coming-

ons.

a) Go-ahead

signals

his blood-
charging

Hotspurred
instinctual

non-stop
s.

b) Breathing-

spell as when
the panting

horses lather
ed and water

ed-down for
on-going

self-renewal
s.

c) Goal-in

sight near
ing one's

continual
on-coming

no-wheres-
but-now.

Unforget

ably there
as if only

dreamed
through the

tideless
flow of in

stinctual
play-back

s.

Childhood

train-stop
Albany-at-

night consum
ing vacantly-

intense dark
nesses.

a) Over-night

change-of-wea
ther cooling-

down interior
light-pause

s.

b) In Germany

where summer
has weather

ed his Scars
dalian lush

ly-sensed
abundance

s.

c) When adverti

zing craftful
sy re-worded

unchange
able appear

ances.

d) She became

fashionably
dressed-up

in her unden
iable sense

of self-be
longing.

e) Education

only sinks-
down its own-

sense of a
continu

ing other
wiseness.

f) A. B.

newly re-fash
ioned in a

thousand-
dollar-an-

hour ivy-
league com

pleteness.

Sirmione

An indefin

able close
ness in the

air when
time seem

s resolute
ly shadow

ing.

The Elephant (*Bressanone*)

a hotel
wooded in the

echoing de
signs of late

medieval time-
enchantment

s.

Time-lengths *(7)*

a) that rainy-

indefinite
day feeling

for a spacious
light-free

time-length.

b) On the road

taking us
down to route

s of its own
pre-forming

time-length
s.

c) Mountain

ous interval
s of increas

ingly shadow
ing depthed–

uncertaint
ies.

d) Our room

balconied
with a view

of pre–destin
ed histori

cal time-
length

s.

e) Here in South

Tirol (if in
tuned to the

same cultural
time-length

s) Oswald v.
Wolkenstein

and Leonhard
Lechner awaken

ed the first
instinctual

prompting
s of that

great German
musical

revival.

f) Here in

this densely
forsaken re

gion we've
become pinna

cled to the
increasing

heights of
untold expand

ing time–length
s.

g) Still in

waiting the
levelling

descent to
those light–

imbuing Ital
ianate time–

length
s.

Furnished

here in the
genuine self-

accomodating
leisure of

this roomed-
in time-

piece.

These Tirolean

hills climb
ing up the

due-length
of my time-

impending
thought-

length
s.

When the inter

play of word
s create

s a mosaic
of timeless

expressive
ness.

"The Rest is

Silence" (Shakespeare)

when these tide
less waves have

smoothed our
time's self-re

deeming need
for blood-re

leasing.

Debussy'

s (very late)
Cello Sonata

modernist
ically out–

balancing
its overtly

abstracted
sound–current

s.

One could

    still feel
    the rains

    had passed
    this night

    through–clean
    sing for morn

    ing's blue-imagin
    ings.

The jagged

    rhythmic in
    undation

    s of Beethoven'
    s late Cello Son

    ata only peace
    fully respon

    sive through
    the encircl

    ing intimacie
    s of its e

    ternally–in
    voking slow–

    down move
    ment.

Those myster

> ious lights at
> the other side
>
> of the lake
> as if calling
>
> into the
> time-conceal
>
> ing mountain
> ous region
>
> s beyond.

Morning

> calm the boat
> s harbour
>
> ed to those
> untold dark
>
> nesses of
> dreamed-re
>
> verie
> s.

A stillness

> surfacing
> the lake's
>
> outspread
> ing quietude
>
> s.

Tiny spider'

> s intricate
> ly vacant
>
> web–arous
> ings.

Where has

> the lake bott
> omed its re
>
> sidue of time
> less calling
>
> s.

Mountain

> s as those
> depth–enclos
>
> ing Macbeth
> ian forest
>
> s moving in
> sistently
>
> nearer.

Years of con

> tinual return
> as the moon–
>
> tide's magnet
> ic claim
>
> s.

As that lone

> ly bird circl
> ing its morn
>
> ing's cloud
> ful expanse.

Waves con

> tinually call
> ing through
>
> their claim
> s of a season
>
> ally recurr
> ing advance.

Sparrow'

s short–stopp
ed hop-timed

advancing in
terval

s.

Weeping

willow's mot
ionlessly

cascading
sadness

es.

Form-feel'

s instinct
ive word-se

curing.

Settling-

> down the blood-
> currents of
>
> oft self-a
> rousing
>
> fears.

Early-blossom'

> s falling color
> s not yet
>
> fully-ripen
> ed to their
>
> pre-forming
> stainless
>
> descent.

Pure music'

> s the true
> measure of
>
> its own real
> ized meaning –
>
> what need for
> anything more!

Kafka

esque dream
s a no-where

s-out of
nothing-left-

to-be-found.

Sun-drugg

ed lizard
untouchab

ly heavy-
weighted

a heat-absorb
ing motion

lessness.

a) The Leopard'

s "70 useless
years" left

him with no
answers left

except my-own
love-center

ed time-ex
posure

s.

b) Who became

that end–
time young

lady guiding
him Dante

esque through
death's un

fathomable
darkness

es.

c) Why read

the aftermath
when the Leo

pard's dying–
out the last

of the Selina'
s inbred in

signiad in
tention

s.

Italian

ate's light
summerly

blue's time-
escaping.

The thorough

> ly secluded
> board-walk
>
> shadowed
> the foot-step
>
> ped lengths
> of his in
>
> tuned echo
> ings.

Sleep a

> wakens a half-
> conscious o
>
> ther-timed
> twilight
>
> world's fath
> omed-imagin
>
> ings.

These dreary

mood-invoking
cloudful day

s left
brightly pre-

attuned sun-
umbrella

s lowered-
down half-

mast.

a) If "there'

s-no-words-
for it"

left A. B.
speechless

ly wide-ey
ed.

b) "Unbeliev

able" Allan

superlat
ived a mon

dane world
of Ivy-league

down-to-earth
correct

ness.

For just a

>short-moment
>he felt a
>
>child-like
>instinct for
>
>upholding
>his colored
>
>balloon's
>spontaneous
>
>redness.

Cutting-the-

>grass-down to
>a nicely-scent
>
>ed even-time
>d closely-a
>
>dept finish.

The after

taste of The
Leopard left

him (as it pro
bably should)

with a some
what less–satis

fying feeling
for its death–

disguis
ing aroma.

This hotel'

s peaceful
ly shadow

ed lake-view
intimate

ly self-con
tent.

The lake'

s cool fresh
ly-bodied

time-encom
passing water

s.

Beyond the

rock-enclosure
s a house of

evil-intent
in the dark

of that moon
ful night un

touchably-si
lent.

The swan

inevitably
self-satisfy

ing as a beau
teously re

fined lady'
s reclusive-

sense of self-
superior

ity.

At the brief

urge of one-
and-a-half a

big step up
or down tenta

tively time-
holding.

When the

gentle flow-
of-waves

softly intun
ed the recurr

ing feeling
of time-for

gotten sadness
es.

Mother

ducks apprec
iably inhabit

a collective
sense for

count-down re
sponsibilit

ies.

Something

darkly secret

ive about the
concealing

depth of her
indwelling

eyes.

Tommy seem

s now even
smaller as

if a sadness
had over-taken

his life of self
less time-ser

ving.

Her eye

s outshone
their pre-or

dained bright
ness as if o

ver-asking a
question

able self-re
assurance.

A self-indul

gent society
dulled from

the efficient
use of conver

sational wit
and an occas

ional bright
ly–lit wis

dom.

The lake

lightly sur
facing its

time–escap
ing morning

reverie
s.

Time's

once again
contently sub

dued from the
torrential

rains of its
increasing

ly unremem
bered past–

tense.

Only "dead

souls" could
safely inhabit

a world so
rich in time-

elusively
contrast

ing uncertain
ties.

Sport-aesthetics (5)

a) Soccer at-its-

best time–or
iented spac

e(d)–speed re
defining thor

ough–going
efficienc

ies.

b) The spac

ious aesthet
ic of golf'

s summer–in
dwelling dis

tantly–evolv
ing green

s.

c) Tennis more

time–condensed
to closer–

ranged tense–
awareness

es.

d) Leisure

ly swimming
the watering

blue's sound–
escaping mo

mentary plea
sures.

e) Kayaking

through the
uneven water

s of those
time–disturb

ing light–
swells.

Only Christ

because
there's no

other love–
encompass

ing forgive
ness of life'

s cruelly
self–impos

ing time–
spans.

Pin-wheel

ing the wind'
s self-en

chanting ex
pressive

ness.

After Schnitz

ler's sub-con
scious anti-

thesis and
Pirandello'

s end-of-cath
arsis-road

Freud's left
little room

to squirm
about his

"scientific"
conjecture

s.

Leaf-trans

cending sound
s transpar

ently awaken
ing.

After the

rains cool
shadows in

habiting
his color

lessly flow
ered sensibil

ities.

Emptied

pleasure
s distanc

ing from
their sound

lessly intun
ed self-suffi

cience
s.

Early morn

ing sparrow
s hip-hopp

ing their
cork-screwed

querulous
down-beat

promptitu
des.

This placid

> morning's
> expressive
>
> ly uneased
> from the night'
>
> s repeatedly
> conclusive
>
> storm–upheav
> als.

Speechless

> couples thought
> fully self-in
>
> habiting
> their own un
>
> spoken silen
> ces.

From a lone

> distance she
> could see if
>
> she'd been
> seen as if
>
> space had be
> come prettily
>
> self-dissolv
> ing.

Octopied

scholars tenta
cled to the

far-range
possibilit

ies of truth-
entangling di

versitie
s.

Poetr

ies seeded
with the pre-

historic vast
ness of torren

tial rain-for
ests.

Picasso

rarely second-
looked me to

a depth-con
suming reapprai

sal.

Little Venetian Harbor *(16 c Desenzano)*

A quiet e

loquence as
if time had

enclosed this
inlet-port

with but limit
ed interior

reflection
s.

Church bell

s attuning
this Christ-

forgotten
time to all

those pre-con
ceived light-

awakening
s.

Retiring

into a self-
satisfying

life of indol
ent leisure

brings on the
earliest sym

ptoms of a pre–
death untime

ly exposure.

Half-moon

hanging the
morning sky

as a hand
less kite per

petually sourc
ing its own e

lusive forget
fulness.

He left an

inescapable
impression

of a brood
ing bird's

supremely
amassed ruff

led feather
s.

When the

sound of
these word

s measure
s its care

fully attun
ed phrased-

meaning
s.

When soccer

becomes a-way-
of life

perpetually
round(ing)

into an
ever-revolving

world-view.

When there'

s nothing left
to see the in

terior claim
s of these e

ver-present
indwelling

darkness
es.

a) As his fath

er always one-
step-ahead

of these
time-escap

ing day
s.

b) As his fath

er restless
ly in-need

of a love-
refurnish

ing home.

c) As his fath

er ever-for
getful of

what's contin
ually time-e

voking its
own self-ap

parent aim
lessness.

d) As his fath

er put-off
by loud o

ver-sized
impact-wo

men.

e) As his fath

er reflect
ively sens

ing those
timeless

after–ech
oes.

f) As his fath

er cut–down
to the essent

ially relev
ant message.

When Bourge

ois well–too–
do–iveness

rounds–out
an over–weight

ed post–middle–
age(d) woman

ly ponder
ousness.

When small

children
ball–play

their color
ing finger'

s intuitive-
design

s.

Juliette

Does her on
coming death

as the autumn
al coloring

of leave
s pre-form

an aura of
transcenden

tal beauty.

Kafka'

s not to be
"understood"

as it's "un
derstand

able" only
in its own

self-deviat
ing process-

of-becoming.

These in

transit time
s-of-our

only stopp
ing for a

momentary
breath-hold.

Early morn

ing conscious
ness slowly pre

vailing as
clouds melt

ing those dis
tantly encom

passing time–
awared

mountain
ranges.

Therapist

s often mirr
oring other

s as a mean
s of identify

ing their own
secretly-es

pying self-re
flection

s.

At 90 my fath

er's "I'm not
old" as if

such persuas
ive power

s could re
time those

plentitude-
of-years

from their e
ven-spoken

course.

a) Attractive

young ladie
s (as with

the aging
Goethe) can

still arouse
a time-enchant

ing spell.

b) Writing-

it-off as if
paper could a

live again
that flesh-

and blooded
ness.

Spider's in

>completed net
>as if taste

>could so–grad
>ually realize

>its pre–con
>ceiving end.

Rough wave

>s intently pre
>vailing o

>ver their
>self-conceal

>ing bottom
>less depth.

She possess

>ed all that a
>vailing charm

>of a moment
>ary light–

>wave.

a) The heal

ing-art of
living-it–

past all
those time-en

during wound
s.

b) No one's

safe (as if
we'd ever

been) shield
ing from

time's abruptly-
abrasive hurt

ings.

Moon-growth

flowers upearth
ed their light–

calling qualit
ies.

That tiny

little boy
innocent

ly pebbling
the water

s with his
own imperman

ent fall.

Braided-

hair's tight–
hold of its

instinctive
ly light–

free finding
s.

German and

Jew two gift
ed people

s blemish
ed with the

stigma of a

deeply–im
pressed Cain–

like indelib
le past.

Lizard

ing these
cool stone

s with thin
lines of

scarcely es
caping shad

ows.

Where do

these time-
wingèd bird

s die in
those dense

ly secluded
thickets

birth-sourc
ed.

"J'accuse" (11)

a) They taught

us to hate
killing the

last drop of
compassion

milked from
our mother'

s life-spend
ing breast

s.

b) They slept

with their in
nocent famil

ies conceal
ing the weap

ons of their
wrathful-re

venging claim
s we'd been

the real child-
killer

s.

c) Life mean

s nothing to
them (their

s or our
s) martyr

s to a de
monic cause.

d) What-kind-of-

God satisfy
ing the blood–

thirst of his
self–chosen

disciple
s.

e) As the world

stood–aside
again quietly

accepting
the demise of

those "upstart
Jews".

f) Their grand

children
claimed for

a–fresh–start
blaming the re

membrance of
their disown

ed victim
s.

g) Their famil

ies cultured-to-
his-finger-tip

s piano teach
er 1933 took

to the-other-
side-of-the

street paved
with the super

iority of a
"master race".

h) They'll al

ways need a
blood–consol

ing sacrifice
for their own

self–satisfy
ing pedestall

ed–ends.

i) He awoke

to the dream
ed-rape of

a one-time
school-mate

who shot that
predator

out of his
own self-en

during shame.

j) Spies in

your own liv
ing-room

listening
in on your

private tele
phone in the

sanctified
name of pro

tecting their
freedom-lov

ing society.

k) "It's all

for-your-own
good" at the

end grave-yard
ing into neat

rows of all–
too-wish

ful-thinking.

Pin-wheel

ing the circuit
ous realms of

wind–color
ing fantasie

s.

Little girl'

s tidying
sense of mine'

s–here–and
nowheres-

else.

"Let's forget

that" 's re
peated imaging'

s recurring
time-sense.

Bare-skull

ed tattooed
skin's abras

ive use of a
new-found

upright man
liness.

Dog-culture

leashed to
a lesser

sense of
child-like i

magining
s.

Sail boat'

s wind–still
interlude

s a slow–move
ment episodic

dream–spell.

When Jewish

self–criticism
becomes an

almost semi–
masochist

ic longing
for a revenge

ful response.

One could

feel that age-
difference

in his over-
timely weight

ed sit-down
ness and her

trying to ap
pear younger

than she con
siderably

need-have-
been.

Sicily *(7)*

a) a "nation"

dead-asleep
from centur

ies of an e
ver-changing

time-growth
world where

its past-
time "hero

s" seldom bred
from its in

digenous
ly ashed-down

soil.

b) a "people"

multi-cultur
ed to a time

less inertia.

c) Mt. Etna

symbol of a
"people"

emotional
to a height

of self-dis
tinctive

ground-swell
ing tidal

instinct
s.

d) a lawless

society secure
ly escounced

in the embell
ished unease

of daily pre-
assuming

self-satisfac
tions.

e) where arti

facts of cul
ture edifying

the lost hori
zons of a

once time–
thriving

past.

f) Its Chris

tian family-o
riented con

servative
values but ten

tatively hold
ing together

a frayed de
caying untime

ly social
fabric.

When science

(or scholar
ship) achieve

s a dormant
consensus

of opportune
ideological

under–current
s.

a) Fausse-reprise

(à la Haydn)

when a single
oft unassum

ing tone bass
oon–like can

re–direction
a symphonic

interlude to its
pre–determin

ed harbour
ing course.

b) a singly

rightly–sens
ed word can

poetize a
prosaical

ly–weighted
design to the

finality of
its spid

er–webbed com
pletion.

These finely–

sensed wind'
s light–air

ed transpar
encie

s.

Seemed (4)

a) "As you like

it" may seem
(at time

s) better–
met than per

sonally pre–con
ceived.

b) A Magritte'

s hatless
man would

seem nakedly
beholden to

a time-length
ening sky-

view.

c) A heat

that melt
ed his thought

s into
stream

s of dream
ed-rever

ies.

d) The psycho-

nets can be
come as all-

entangling
as the spider'

s web's no-way
s-out.

Realising Truths *(11)*

a) A good novel

can person
ally live

times remain
for the histori

ian paper–
weighted from

their heart–
minded reach.

b) Poems can

help us real
ize what we

seem to have
sensed surfac

ing express
ively self–

exposing.

c) Realism

realize
s only the

imprinted
(though

shadowless)
time–sense.

d) Poetic

"understand
ing" can'

t be trans
lated as an

estimable
bridge into

a prosaic
idea-sheme.

e) Beauty real

izes itself
as if time

lessly pre
conceived.

f) Genius is

less a per
sonal gift

transcend
ing its imman

ently self–
disguising

origin
s.

g) Post-classi

cal late Beet
hoven often

rhythmical
ly pattern

s an open–
ended self–

perpetuat
ing time–

sequence.

h) When excess

ively unrefin
ed emotion as

in Mendelssohn'
s op. 80 Quartet

override
s his essent

ially self-ef
ficient form–

defining
sense.

i) (and yet)

Schubert's
ever-repet

itive beauti
fying interval

s us aesthet
ically still

mostly self–
satisfying.

j) Haydn's

spontaneous
ly evocative

wit seldom
dries–us down

to scholast
ically repetit

ive know-it–
alls.

k) Mozart

in minor oft
moods–us in

to stream
s of self–

reflective
sadness

es.

When butter

    flies born off-
    balancing

    a need for
    steadfast

    fluttering
    s.

    a) These dis

    tant hills cur
    ving into

    the length of
    a soundless

    momentary
    illusion.

    b) Italian

    ate warmth
    personing

    the length
    and depth of

    one's own
    phantom

    ly-obscur
    ed self-be

    ing.

c) If it was

only at Mardi
Gras when one

becomes mask
ed to the

fictive illus
ions of an i

maginary self-
being.

Sun-down

time-releas
ing the lake'

s surfac
ing light

nesses.

A child'

s looking-up
at her father'

s looking-down
at their own

self-shadow
ings.

A little-

sensed girl
dressed in

polka-dott
ed region

s of color
ing self-ex

pressive
ness.

These time-

withholding
sun-down mo

ments tensed
an indistinct

self-aware
ness.

Sisters (2)

a) A denial of

a life that
wasn't her

s to lead a
self-image

of their
not-mine.

b) A retreat

into the up
stairs of a

world of un
resolving

ly closed-
offs.

The father

so much more
of himself

an initia
tive that

couldn't be
kept for hold

ing itself
back.

The mother

more of a
beautify

ing child-
like image

mirroring
his own self-

securing succ
esses.

The unreveal

ing patience
of a touch-

told spider
webbed in a

not-now even-
then other

wiseness.

He seemed

so official
ly clothed

in an attit
ude of self-

attuned re
sponse that

not even an
off-side

remark could
unease the

time-endur
ing claim

s of his al
ways self-re

assuring com
posure.

The first

hesitant
ly respons

ive touch of
this softly

expressive
morning's air

ed him into
a spacious

ly preconcei
ved beyond

ness.

Desenzano

the silent
city across

the lake
self-encom

passing cen
turies of time

less remembr
ances.

Rain-time

umbrella
s upholding

the inside-
out of sun–

shine appear
ance

s.

a) The touch-

lightness of
Italianate

flower's trans
parently sensed–

awakening
s.

b) The dark

ly mooned
voice of

North-tim
ed flower's

almost re
sonating

fear.

Her hard-

masculine
straight-for

ward look as
a red-brick

house fully
fortified.

Stream-

lined cloud
s releasing

the delicate
whiteness

of early morn
ing reverie

s.

Some of

these poem
s could be

come unduly
dense heavily

color
ed as much

of the late
indwelling

Brahms.

Free-find

ing feeling
s as a child

with his
wind-color

ing kite.

Those sus

picious of o
thers' motive

s would be
best-off mir

roring their
own.

Carefree

moods as when
the shadow

s had been
taken-out of

his existent
ial fear

s.

The transpar

ent depth of
that unspok

en moon kept
watching o

ver the night'
s tidal dark

nesses.

Mattia

an always-
smiling baby

as if life
had become

but a play-
thing of his

unknown se
cretly confid

ing pleasure
s.

Gaia

his sister
at two-and-

a-half care
fully stepp

ed-measur
ed a distance

away from
darkly with

holding stran
gers.

An early morn

ing stillness
softly awaken

ing these
quietly reflec

tive infold
ing hill

s.

He only met

> the breathed-
> silence of his
>
> self-seclud
> ed voice
>
> outside this
> restless
>
> ly night-im
> pulsing
>
> city.

Have some

> persons taken-
> on (for him)
>
> the continu
> ously self-
>
> revealing
> extent of pre
>
> viously un
> chartered
>
> city-limit
> s.

No one can

    measure the
eye-depth

    length of
this self-con

    cealing lake.

The in-bred

    depth of an a
bused child

    as the self-
withholding

    shame of part
ially lamed

    creature
s.

At Salò

    one could al
most feel

    the silent
ly in-coming

    boat water
ed from a

    soundless
view.

The Crucifixion *(Salò 1449)*

"It is fulfill
ed" Crucifix

ion at Salò
became so in

timately per
sonal that I

almost felt
as if He were

hung there
vastly alone

just–for–me.

Be careful

for every word
every thought

It's known
it's heard

you'll be tra
ced–down e

ven the scent
will find–you–

out.

It got in

couldn't get
out swimming

(at first)
carefree

then despar
ately closed–

in to a no-
escape route.

After the

storm a fresh
ly awaken

ing breeze
s innocent

ly sun-lit
express

iveness.

He claimed

it was a new–

start newly–
born though

the rhythmic
pulse of his

very–being e
ver–so–con

stantly self–
inhabiting.

She changed

so often her
colored table–

cloth's spec
ially designed

patterns that
at times I be

gan to wonder
what she'd so

prettily been
covering–o

ver.

Unwanted Stranger

He common

ly slept-off
his self-in

habiting
dreams but

this one so
often recurr

ed as an un
wanted strang

er habitual
ly knocking

at his lock
ed and bolt

ed door.

Language

has become
my servant

At age 10

or 11 he ran
more with his

facial express
ion protrud

ing arm-length
ed an unseen

(and yet)
self-suspend

ing goal.

Mirror

ing water'
s transpar

ently succ
essive sky-

length.

For Rosemarie'

s softness
feels me to

a genuine
ly express

ive self-
guarantee.

Gaza

city of doom
ed blood-trap

tunnels a dark
ening feared

under-world
rat-looming

creature
s death-arm

ed.

Fields of

clover out
spreading the

wind's light-
enhancing

timeless
ly sensed-

calling
s.

They don't

really care
if their own

children die
as human shield

ing their true
martyr

dom blood–lick
ed to their

helpless
ly mourned

victim
s.

a) A ceremon

ial process
ion of cloud

s this early
morning as if

held within
their own rever

ential silenc
es.

b) A scarce

ly breath
ed all–pre

vading still
ness.

c) as if sound

itself had

become but
an echoing

self–reflect
ion.

d) These waves

but bare
ly touch

ed soundless
ly called.

e) The forgott

en moon hidd
en behind

its own soul
ful intent.

f) Ducks sur

facing the
unknown depth

s of a bottom
less deep.

g) These thin

ly self-dis
guising cloud

s veiling
but a self-

apparent
celestial

calm.

Beethoven'

s dramatic
vein's oft

too hard-
tensed for

my supple e
vocative

ly lyrical
sensibil

ity.

An insistent

ly sound-pro
voking soc

iety seems
to have lost

its innate
sense of in

terior space-
invoking si

lence
s.

(after Pirandello)

Here and now
it's but one

author search
ing-out the

possibility
of a recept

ively sensit
ized audience.

Bikini

young bodies
on–display–

for–all rais
ing elder men'

s eyes to a
thorough–go

ing height
of touch and

consuming
not the least

of a private
intimately–

withholding
sense left.

One shouldn'

t blame one'
s long dead

father for
having taken–

over some of
his residual

ly self–perpet
uating weak

nesses.

Sirmione'

s two-tim
ed castled

city's half-
blind camera

ed tourist
s medieval

ly-poised
timeless

ly-aware.

White gull

s peaceful
ly gliding

the winds im
perceptive

ly near.

a) When the

words don't
come quite

right as a
slightly

out-of-focus
long-time

friendship.

b) When that

newly color
ing dress

failed to
match her

subtlely
self–inclin

ing smile.

c) Family-

friendly

intimate
ly self–con

fining hotel
transiting

on–the–way
imperson

ally–styled
tourist

s.

d) Wild-eyed

night–roving
moon–intense

ly animall
ed to a per

sistently
slowed–down

caged–in
existence.

e) Haydn or

Beethoven'
s mid–life

crisis' less
ening urge

for innovat
ive upstart

s.

f) That time

less kind-of–
day when e

ven waiting
seems inopport

unely self-ex
posing.

a) Dark day'

s vast expanse
of impending

shadowing
forgetful

ness.

b) When these

summer–ripen
ed leaves

hang heavily
self–consum

ing.

c) When the

air's dense
ly enclosing

an all–fore
boding near

ness.

d) Even fear

seems untouch
ably near.

e) Where are those

wide-perspect
ives all-

spacing
sensed-light

ness
es.

f) Darkly self-

inhabiting
birds the

sky's lessen
ing reach.

g) Those house

s across the
street seem

mutely ines
capably

there.

h) These are

the times
of dream'

s shadow
ing con

scious
ness.

i) Writing-it-

off as if e
rasing the

uncovered
guilt from Miss

Blackburn's 2nd
grade black

board.

He's on his

>   high-horse a
>   gain saddled
>
>   to the self-
>   consuming
>
>   depth of Men
>   achem Mendel'
>
>   s unlimited
>   perspect
>
>   ives.

Those dark

>   ly-colored
>   time-recurr
>
>   ing sound
>   s of Marin
>
>   Marais' life-
>   pulsing gamba
>
>   suite
>   s.

If there'

>   s no-other-
>   way-to-say-
>
>   it then say-
>   it-now!

The first

movement of
Bartók's 5th

Quartet storm
ed me under–

cover of
what's more–

to–come.

Rosemarie

that yester
day's feel-of–

you through
over 50 year

s of alway
s–now.

3 times Macke (3)

a) When Macke

fades his
colors in

to the ob
scurity of

light's af
tershine.

b) When he ach

ieves an almost

certainty
of upright–

clarity.

c) smudgy

indistinct
as if his

vision had
become color

lessly phas
ed-out.

a) Womanly

ideal (as
with Beatrice

and the ob
scurely-sens

ed Laura)
pedestall

ed to a
height of

untouch
able purity.

b) You're for

real Rosemarie
not more than

you really
are imperfect

ly-mine.

Did the in

securing route
s of Dante'

s exile init
iate a self–

revealing
guide to his

cosmologi
cal path-find

ings.

Is personal

love (as with
Dante and

Donne) but a
platonic

ally pre-sens
ed imaging

of the more-
fully self-

encompass
ing realm

s of Christ'
s divine love.

Great epic *(for Warren)*

"poetry"
(as that of

Dante's or
Milton's)

at especial
ly breath

ed-down mo
ments release

a lyrical
voice as a

beautified
bird from its

unlocked cage.

Are the

> flesh and
> blood–stream
>
> s of sensual
> love more
>
> birth-giving
> or (as some
>
> poets would in
> sist) death–in
>
> habiting.

Always-there

> (as Hotspur)
> before the
>
> pre–given
> timing it to
>
> his own in
> stinctual
>
> necessit
> ies.

Are we all

exiled here
(Dantesque)

from the still
haunting taste

of life's per
manently as

piring death–
route

s.

Predecessors

We all come
from some place

(even Shakes
peare) pre–

forming his
no-wheres–

place to
only-now.

Beatrice contra Dante

What woman

wants to be
loved for

what she isn'
t. Take me

down from
that timeless

pedestal
Open your e

yes to the
here-I-am.

There are no

pre-condition
s for great

art calls
whom it hear

s (perhaps)
from the bond'

s of his "mas
ter's" pre-form

ing time-
growth.

The arts

rarely "corres
pond" (impression

istic France
or the great

Chinese multi-
masters)

seeks their
own time-length

ed self-express
iveness.

There's a de

gree of person
al evil (as

with Wagner
and Rimbaud)

that contamin
ates me from

even their
finest artist

ic design
s.

Most personal *(10)*

a) On the pri

soner's block
time-awaiting

that all-im
pending

death-call.

b) Lover'

s code-word
s identify

ing what's
become of

those most per
sonal intima

cies only-
their

s.

c) Pre-teen

girl's private
diary writt

en-out but
secretly un

disclosing.

d) Those up

stair's room
s under lock

and keyed-
off to a lost

timeless
ness.

e) Moment

s of clear
ing-to-voice

from the crowd'
s emerging

shadow
s.

f) Only Neil re

members
what I've long-

since forgott
en freshly

realized.

g) The first

sensed-touch
of a woman'

s mind-form
ing body.

h) When the

morning slow
ly encompass

ing its in
dwelling

light.

i) Snow-drop

s piercing
that appar

ent white of
its pre–design

ing innocen
ce.

j) When the

flow–of–bird
s rediscover

ing world
s of untold

soundless
ness.

Trees ar

rayed to such
a time–impend

ing height
that those

spaced–distan
ces seemed

as if eclips
ed forgott

en altogeth
er lost.

Some mistake

s can be
safely put-a

side forgott
en but this

one kept re
curring at

the heart of
his very be

ing couldn'
t possibly

bleed–itself–
out.

Too early

At the end
of July first

leaves yellow
ed dried–down

to the depth
of death's im

pending call.

a) Is aesthet

ic sensibil
ity a part

of a process
of self-be

coming or is
it pre-given

as our eye'
s and ear'

s own person
al sense of

self-selectiv
ity.

b) Why do we

seem to hear
some work

s so similar
ly and o

thers as if
the music it

self had be
come so dis

tinctly o
therwise

voiced.

c) If The Lord

created
through the

unique call
of his irre

sistible word
why has see

ing become
the origin

of our own
expressib

ly-why.

d) When Wallace

Stevens poet
ized me at

age 15 was
it his voice

I'd been hear
ing or a

faint echo
of my own

muted-self.

It rained

the night
through and

yet the in
visible

moon remain
ed so un

touchab
ly dream-a

wake.

This window

ever-so-fine
ly touched

with the dark
ening rain'

s precise
time-recall

ings.

This rail

ing's steel-
shine cool

ed the very-
distanc

ing of his
intouched

self-sensibil
ities.

a) His night

ly self-inhab
iting darkness

es day-clear
ed by but a

small vase'
s lightly

flowering
express

ive-moment
s.

b) Haydn

always managed
to brighten-

up the impend
ing depth of

his daily self-
awareness

es.

c) a tiny

bird's wing
èdly unveil

ing color-
find

s.

Some poem

s as womb-
misplaced em

bryos not
such an easy-

birth.

Snailing

A small unob
strusive

snail but
half-way-up

a distance
it hardly

had been anti
cipating.

When the

air's heavy
with the time-

telling weight
of unquest

ionable silen
ces.

Dr. Schimpf'

s owl uplift
ing eyes the

way a school-
principal as

himself vivid
ly assesses

the implicat
ions of a far-

reaching de
cision.

That same un

      spoken room
      not yet a

      wakened from
      the dark of

      its self-en
      closing si

      lence
      s.

A word-

      too-many tipp
      ed the balan

      ce as at sea
      waves off-

      centering.

A poetry

(especially
in a world

of hate and
despair)

that denie
s whatever

claims for a
beauty even

momentar
ily self-sus

taining.

Even those

time–attend
ing mountain

s self-support
ing the dried-

down flow of
perpetual

light–instin
cts.

When Petrarch

as the first
mountain-

climbed the
fresh-aware

ness of his
only-now.

Even if

Petrarch'
s Laura was

more imagin
ed than the

flesh-and-
blood of a

realized
womanly more

than Dante'
s mind-ascend

ing sacredly-
espoused

Beatrice.

This country

road elongat
ed even beyond

my mind's
lengthened

view of hidd
en seclusive

darkly wood
ed interior

enclosure
s.

a) Benn at

his best signi
fies the mind-

sense to the
word's intrin

sically poet
ic-confine

s.

b) Those who

realize Brecht
as a major

poet have
depthed–lost

their mood-
feel for

what's intrin
sically poet

ic.

c) Rilke'

s "thing-
poems" articu

lately word-
precise what'

s so oft with
him more evocat

ively–suggest
ive.

d) Trakl

still remain
s for me

too heavily
word–weight

ing down a
depth of

self–express
ive coloring

intense–feel
ings.

e) Else Lasker-

Schüler as
usual equipp

ed with exot
ically fantast

ic imagery
heavily e

vocative
ly pre–ton

ed inviting.

You can'

 t shield your
 self from death

 not even from
 that middle-in-

 the-road-o
 pen-eyed fully-

 intact squirrel'
 s out-jumped

 his remain
 ing earthly

 pleasure
 s.

Pain embedd

 ed in his skele
 tal bones shut-

 off much of
 his night-

 time easily-
 contented

 selved-
 pleasure

 s.

When an art

ist's so per
sonally affect

ed he's usually
at the height

of his most in
timate-genuine

form – Tele
mann in his

Pimpinone
wasn't.

This morning

re-scened the
expressive

blue of Rose
marie's time-

intending
smile.

Rhapsody

Fields of
fully-ripen

ed wheat and
corn nourish

ing the touch-
feel of these

soft wind'
s through-en

compassing
(though

lightly sens
ed) imagin

ings.

Thought-

poems as if
the poem

could think
more than

it's simply
being-there.

Looking

through dis
tances as if

time could
be brought

closer-to(o).

Up or down

Do we grow
up to the

self-certain
ty of our

most distin
guishing

self or down
from that

spontane
ous child–

like other
wiseness.

a) A field of

wild flower
s spontan

eously cele
brating their

pre-forming
color-find

s.

b) Rows of

articulate

ly cultivat
ed roses re

minding of
fully self–

conscious
carefully at

tired young
ladies.

c) Not the

need for lang
uage itself

can become
artificial

ly groomed
for a choice-

selective
properly at

tiredness.

d) Truly classi

cal signifie
s increasing

ly more than
that most–

finished
polished–up

generally
self–satisfy

ing appear
ance.

Season

s-of-the-
mind cycling

around a rhy
thmically

imprecise
sense of con

tinual self-
persuasion

s.

Answering Einstein

There's no
possible formu

la for redis
covering a

God hidden with
in His own

self-preclud
ing darkness

es.

On the late Haydn

Untouchable
beauty in

stincts an
unfathomed

desire for a
thoroughly

accomplish
ed self-com

pletion.

It's the

naturally
sustain

ing polarity
of man and

woman that
axis a thor

oughly complet
ed unity of

self-being.

What's out-

of-bounds
may still flow

er a singular
sense of rari

fied beauty.

Times may

weather some
into an un

deniable mould
of perpetual

sameness.

Before you

flower a beau
tified young

lady reconsid
er the full

scope of her
mother's

time-accumu
lating proport

ions.

Moon-rise

>weightless
>ly time-as

>cending.

The wood'

>s darkly
>brooding si

>lence
>s.

At sunrise

>the sky hori
>zoned beyond

>its light-in
>time-glow.

A small-

>phased vase
>kept-close

>to its flow
>ering fore

>sight
>s.

A small

color-intend
ing snail

climbed its
slow-found

way up or
down through

its invisib
ly desirable

hold-ons.

Daniella *(my niece)*

only in after-
math planned-

out her life
had been phas

ed into
chess-board

time-sequenc
es.

Why have

> these picture
> s been so care
>
> fully framed
> to close-in
>
> their time-
> withhold
>
> ing appear
> ances.

Pisanello'

> s (in Rome)
> young lady
>
> at a side-
> glanced den
>
> sity of facial
> ly-formed ex
>
> pressive
> ness.

Truth's

> often left sus
> pending bet
>
> ween there
> and now time-
>
> tensioned.

Illmensee *(August 3) (10)*

a) Wave-drift

ing through a

world of time
lessly lost

appearance
es.

b) The lake'

s untold depth
but a measure

of our secret
ly inhabit

ing remembran
ces.

c) The wood'

s withhold
ing these

time–secur
ing darkly

intensed
shadow

ings.

d) Time-chang

ing cloud-e
volving mo

mentary un
certaint

ies.

e) Your muted

voice lost
in these e

choing silen
ces.

f) Thunder her

alding a med
ieval knight

ly-evoked pro
cessional.

g) Fear as

arrows rain
ing precise

ly sharpen
ing wounded-

instinct
s.

h) A moment

ary ease of
time-phas

ing inter
ludes.

i) Blue-pleas

ured light-
releasing

s.

j) The hushed

unspoken here-
and-now of

this timeless
ly after-sens

ed.

Döhring

when a wo
man dominate

s a man'
s shyly hidd

en overrid
ing self-poss

essing inter
ests.

If one could

only touch the
fragile scent

of these time-
escaping mo

ments.

Church

bells sound
ing-out a

brighten
ed awareness

of summer'
s light-in

tuned distan
cing

s.

These wood

s darkening
the depth of

his indwell
ing silence

s.

Haydn Sonata

Can finger
s alone pre

cision the
intimate

touch of
such classi

cal intrica
cies.

He princess

ed his daught
er into his

own knightly-
encompassing

persuasive
forebear

ings.

An oriental

carpet woven

into these
bright-color

ing thread'
s time-con

ceiving.

Rosemarie

you've land
scaped much–

of-my-life
with intimate

ly recept
ive shore–

calling
s.

Immovable

morning cloud
s as if time

had become
densely self–

inhabiting.

Those ground-

sensed Indian
s witness

ing their own
echoing time–

beat.

She alway

s felt pre–es
tablished in

to a 2nd–
choice twin–

brother's pri
mary gain.

Spitzweg'

> s butterfly'
> s enlarging
>
> well beyond
> his eye-nett
>
> ing instinct
> ual catch.

Curt Goetz "Ingeborg" (7)

> a) when a pass
>
> ionless "love"
>
> becomes more
> a respectful
>
> need for an
> all-encompass
>
> ing friend
> ship.

> b) when a pass
>
> ionate "love'
> s" more an a
>
> dolescent
> unfulfill
>
> ing flight–
> fantasy.

c) Can a woman

"love" two-
at-once if

only because
she's become

that two-in-
one answer

ing-call.

d) An alcoholic

farce-ending'
s not a way

out but an
entertain

ing means of
begging-the-

question.

e) Has the com

ical aunt's
over-swelling

self-assurance
s become (at

times) (as with
Polonius)

right-down
truth's allur

ing alley-
way.

f) If Goetz

is implying a
three-person

ed love he'
s become as

post–Christian
as our own

decaydent
age.

g) Goetz him

self may be
more a "play

right" than a
"real poet"

but his lang
uage still re

mains intriging
ly persistent.

Summer '14 *(3)*

a) Gaza

Should Israel
be charged

with "war-
crimes" when

attacked to-
be-destroyed

by an enemy
targeting in

nocent civil
ians using

their own as
protective

shield
s.

b) Israel

once again
left alone

as Christ
to a chosen

ness of these
irreconcil

able end-time
s.

c) Once again

on those still-
remembering

German street
s that hate

fully echoing
cry of "death-

to-the-Jews".

"David"

that honey-
combed voice

of hers e
voking an al

most 70 years
lapse with

such over-
brimming

sweetness
es.

Our son

Raphael'

s wide open
spaces a mind

not yet de
ciphering

lost-time
cause

s.

a) Crossed the

border to Ger
many (1961)

feared of
most-every

shadowing
death close-

by my very-
path rest

lessly a
live.

b) Passport

control as if
for that very-

moment I'd be
come state

less imperson
ally there.

c) I knew he'

d have kill
ed me (not

me but the
Jew-image of

my very-self)
16 years ear

lier in his
death-haunt

ing presence.

d) Was it he

really there
or his uni

formed flesh-
and-blood

death-star
ing past.

e) Gaza/Israel

those darkly-
scened tunnel

s deeply hidd
en below their

surfacing un
masked ready-

to-kill death-
haunting pre

sence.

f) 1945 the

7-year-old
Rosemarie flee

ing through
those enclos

ing wooded sha
dows of the

enemy plane
s circling the

guiding path
of her very-

being.

g) Does grass

(as they say)
grow-over

those blood
less dried–

down wound
s now flower

ing an inno
cently unbe

holden-red.

h) And the sur

vivors those
chosen to re

member the
birth of a

death-liv
ing past.

The exact

plot not yet
marked-out

nor the grave-
stone fully-

identified
yet each day

he passes
that silently

possessed
field of his

future encom
passing home.

The cool

ly sensed-feel
of these over

coming water'
s deeply breath

ed time-expos
ures.

a) Sun flower

s a child-
like imitat

ion of their
Father's rad

iantly imman
ent-calling

s.

b) The morn

ing mist se
cretly with

holding the e
vasive silence

s of the moon'
s untimely

after-glow.

c) Morning

mist as a wo
man's unveil

ing intima
cies.

a) Illmensee

wombed in
the encompass

ing depth of
its untold

darkness
es.

b) Illmensee

instinctive
ly reveal

ing the wav
ed-surface

s of life'
s most inti

mate time-
calling

s.

a) The taste-

of–our–time
s seem so–

oft irrelev
antly self–a

bandoning.

b) The taste-

of–our–time
s as an un

ripened
fruit cored

to its dried–
hard center.

Cut flowers (2)

a) Why cut

one's own aes
thetic need

s to time'
s watering

death–withhold
ing stillness

es.

b) when these

wind-timed

fields flow
ing their

own flower
ing rhythm

ic-design.

If questions *(4)*

a) The if-

questions may
not have happ

ened but they
still remain

persistently
alive uneas

ing the very-
source of our

now-being.

b) And what we

left behind
may sudden

ly catch-up
with our care

fully painted-
over house-

façade
s.

c) A bad-con

science may
still dwell at

the gnawing
source of our

most intimate
ly cultivat

ed raison-d'
être.

d) (and yet)

there was no-
other-way-

out of our
past-time

delemmas laby
rinthed in

those daily re
curring fear

s.

For Robert

Thrills
teen-ager

taking the
seat off of

our Playground
ed full-down

bottomless
fears.

As a fox

hidden from
his own self-

exposing color
ings waits

harmlessly
concealed

caught-in-
flight his in

nocently trap
ped victim.

Mozart e

minor Violin
Sonata in two

movement
s yet the min

uet felt–
through a

sadness indel
ibly final

ized.

Bach's Partita

no. 2 d minor

as an ancient
monument

so strongly
almost imper

sonally pre–
conceived

that little
room left to in

habit its
well–forti

fied (though)
roomless ap

pearance
s.

Shostakovich

Piano Trio 2

also person
ally depthed

elegy for a de
parted friend

or a stone-
wrought epi

taph for his
long-suffer

ing heroic
people.

S. L.

cast me as
a time-spared

fortune-child
when he a

depth-wound
ed survivor

of war and
two still time-

haunting in
human regime

s.

S. L.'s

father after
two wars re

mained for
him as but a

paled ghost –
of-a-person

whereas mine
so over-siz

ed towering
above his

self-made i
mage of a

fledging
son.

"Of course"

and "natural
ly" words of

an inspoken
though rare

ly self-quest
ioning author

ity.

a) After rain

when the air'
s clear and

lightly free
s one's own

freshly-tim
ed renewal

s.

b) After rain

when that
fear-inhabit

ing tension'
s left little

of its sur
facing depth

ed release.

For Hans

after 13 year
s of keeping

him by-all-
charitable-

means afloat a
gainst time'

s irresist
able urge

failed.

The Chosen (3)

a) not better

deeper finer

pathless
ly lost to

His repeat
ed go-ahead

signalling
s.

b) Why David

the adulter
ous-murderer

than Jonathan
the eldest son

upholding
his singular

ly-proven
rightly-sens

ed good-in
tention

s.

c) The Church

as St. Peter
Christ-deny

ing surface-
sinking irre

solately
rock-proven.

1914–2014 (3)

a) If man'

s mostly a
ligned again

st his better-
self why didn'

t that shell-
bound-pit com

pletely swall
ow-him-up.

b) "The Idea

of Progress"

depthed well-
below the sur

face of our
own idealized

phantom-i
mage.

c) Have we

ever learned
to follow

those alter
nate route

s to our own
misguided

self-intent
ions.

A soft

ly persuas
ive blue warm

ing the length
and depth of

our sense
for see

ing why.

Her face so

threatenly
darked an in

tensity of un
accountable

design
s.

Picked-flow

ers seem how
ever depthed–

in–color so
fragilely

touched.

The distant

call of bird
s instinct

ively awaken
ed to their

time–impend
ing flight.

Illmensee

lightly sur
faced encirc

led in wave
s of time–

passing in
distinct

ly heard mo
ments.

Each day

darkening
the depth of

night's
time-telling

hold.

A kind of

Mozartean
sadness

lingering
ever-so

transpar
ently a

wake.

And these

rain-drop
window

ing night'
s still

soundless
appearan

ces.

Is even

> the bird's
> song less
>
> depthed from
> its color
>
> ing intonat
> ions.

Rosemarie

> why this
> plaintive
>
> sense-of–
> loss when
>
> our love re
> mains so
>
> securely
> time-hold
>
> ing.

The rain

> s have less
> ened into
>
> a muted
> voice of di
>
> minishing
> whispered–
>
> echoing
> s.

The light

ly touched
phrasing

s of Mendels
sohn's scherzo'

s fleeting re
membrance

s.

a) Those dark

dreams that
leave one

helpless
ly adrift

shoreless
ly time-a

bandoning.

b) Are they

but an unde
ciphered

warning sig
nalling un

told danger
s ahead.

c) Or a threat

ening past
revealing

itself anew
symbolical

ly reawaken
ed.

d) Mounting

as Sisyphus
to the top

of a space
less hold.

e) Or a person

called from
the past to

testify a
gainst one'

s reliably
intact self–

assurance
s.

f) The empt

ied street
s of Malmsheim

echoing a
death-like

closeness.

g) Sermon in-

hand church
so silent

ly waiting
that he stood

to the pulpit
speechless

ly self-appar
ent.

h) The dead

risen again
as but phant

om image
s of one'

s own last judg
ment.

i) A tomb gar

dened with
one's own

name birth
and death-

date indel
ibly inscrib

ed.

j) Trying to

flee as a
frog hypnoti

cally snake-
entranced.

k) Trained

with only
that Jew-star

clothed to
one's flesh

less silenc
es.

l) Lined-up

to be shot–
down to a

grave–immen
sing depth.

m) Gas cham

bered to that
finalized

choked–in
nakedness.

Rough wave

s grasping
these last

watered–
timed uncer

taintie
s.

A woman

reading a
book read

ing back her
thought's in

creasing
ly time-flow

ing.

Water-slide

cooling down
those renew

ed impress
ions of

cloud-appear
ances.

a) Nothing

left to-be-
said a va

cancy of
timed-tens

ion.

b) Nothing-

in–common ex

cept an un
common un

easing aware
ness of much–

the–same.

Tolystoyan

These muted

clouds depth
ed into a

motionless
mosaic of ob

scured causal
ities.

a) Apples

hanging the
untouched

weight of
his linger

ing taste-
find

s.

b) Shopping

the continu
ous temptat

ions of Eve'
s time-impend

curiosity.

A seldom

frog alternate
ly jumped the

rhythmic
pulse of its

spaced-down
contemplat

ions.

Funeralled

a room of si
lently vacant

chairs star
ing-out the

full-length
of solemn

ly emptied
distance

s.

A 15th cent

ury "Last Supp
er" with a

cat (not that
dog-faithful

ness) turn
ing its dis

daining back
to Judas'

traitor
ous behavior.

Envy (5)

a) starts

young the com
parative eye

s of parent
s (not their

s but other
s) levelled

beyond person
al reach.

b) "She's a

straight-A-
student don't

get too near
her cello'

s too valua
ble for your

lower-grade
intention

s."

c) That Mozart-

Salieri "Amad
eus" may have

been fabricated
into the re

curring evil
designs of

our all-too-
human-self.

d) Cain as Esau'

s on the blood-
scent of Abel/

Jacob's home-
bred stead

fast chosen
ness.

e) "Be satisfied

with what you
have" upbrow

ed a self-
satisfying

superior–
pose.

Illmensee

August 14th

40 degree
wake–up

chill bodied
to the bone'

s steadfast
inertia.

The moon

disappear
ed for day

s we sensed
only dull

ed–clouded
precluding

silence
s.

The silver

pheasant
pattern

ed to a melod
ically in

scribed time-
sense.

Big-eared

rabbit's e
longating

instinct
ual sense-

flying
s.

These daily

dark rain
s ominous

ly depthed
to their con

tinuously
untold forebod

ings.

A two-generat

ion divide
uninhabit

ing but a dis
tant blood–

link inescap
ably thinned–

out.

A manicur

ed dressed–
down young

lady thorough
ly scented

to her fine
ly colored

smile-intend
ing finger–

tipped reach.

Are such dis

plays of harm
lessly domest

ically-furr
ed creature

s meant to
tone-down

some children'
s otherwise

unduly aggress
ive behavior.

When summer

lost its ephem
eral name

rained-down in
to bleak re

minders of cool
ly time-disab

ling autum
nal appearan

ces.

Goethe'

s eye-touch
discover

ies in Rome
of a naked

woman's bod
ied his own

instinct
ually arous

ed urging
s.

Smetana's

"From my life"
Quartet left

us serious
ly smiling

at its late
late romantic

over-swell
ing self-in

dulgence
s.

The polka

danced us
right–into

the show–it–
all–self of a

19th century
beer–arousing

entertain
ment hall.

Kurtág's

op. 1,1 Quart
et short–phas

ed an impetu
ous start–

stop all–in
clusive reap

praisal.

Don't give

me that what–
have–you–done–

to–me look
child–like

suspicious
ly hurt.

Immovable

objects as
a marriage

lined-up or
even dug-in

beyond all
interced

ing realmed
neutral

ground.

Road-time

lengths ex
tending the

eye's tran
scient aware

nesses.

If we could

all-at-once
encompass

that room'
s receptive-

imaging
s.

a) Wood hand-

cut in time–
rowed motion

lessly in
tact perform

ances.

b) These hedge

s manicured
with the

fine-touch
of a barber'

s off–hand
ed duly–sens

ed precis
ion.

c) An unharnass

ed watch–dog'
s blood–dead

ly teethed–
incision

s.

Small white

ly-scented
roses self-

enclosing in
timately-

voiced silen
ces.

Sirmione

Brahmsian

These self-
same shadow

s deepening
now into

the reclus
ive depth of

autumn's per
vasively

densed color
ings.

How imper

ceptively
moods change

as cloud
s evasive

ly self-in
volving.

Partners (2)

a) Bikini show-

pieces smil
ing vacant

ly timeful
appearance

es.

b) His upright

manly stature
tattooed to

a steadfast
ly muscled–

culture.

These weep

ing willow
s flowing

into tear
fully light

ened remem
brance

s.

A summer

tree leaf
lessly dead

at the top
as some per
sons I've

known died-
down to their

porously in
ept substan

ce.

a) Birds at

least feather
instinctive

ly colored
time-cause

s.

b) Primitive

ly inhabited
island-people

s at least
God-fearing

all those self-
shadowing im

pending dark
nesses.

a) He looked

much–the–same
if one didn'

t second–look
a darkly re

vealing death–
hold embedded

deeply within
those untouch

able region
s of his

bodied-self.

b) Next year

he won't re
turn only a

stoned–remem
brance in

some remotely
distant place

inscribing
(if only it

could) his
specially e

lusive Austri
an-smile.

When the

fresh scent
of newly o

vened bread a
wakens one'

s eyes to the
first blue of

Italy's frag
rant skie

s.

Personae (2)

a) One couldn'

t quite place–
her beyond

the casual
ly sporting

attire of her
reticently

self–assum
ing smile.

b) Was it

the non–chal

ance of his
mostly self–

sufficient
middle–aged

smile that
stood–him so

carefully–
chosen a

part.

Presences (4)

a) Stone-bottom

ed shores as
if people

with the touch
ed–down claim

s of a once
self–inhabit

ing past.

b) A lone gull

separate
ly situat

ing its wave
d–in pre

sence.

c) Across-the-

lake the morn
ing resolve

of Decenzano'
s light-en

chanting hill-
bred self-as

suming pre
sence.

d) If it al

ways has-to-
be-done your

way you've is
landed an un

inhabited
world with

your self-comm
anding pre

sence.

Glanced *(2)*

a) Eye-glance

talking most
ly inhabit

ing around-
the-other-

way right
ly beside-

the-point.

b) Spark-ham

mered glance

d iron-a
wakening

s.

Dujardin'

s unmistak
able blue

pre-meditat
ing cool-

timed.

a) Thunder

suddenly a

lert to its
struck

sound-
voice.

b) The pier

cing dart-like
flash of light

ning's soul-
streaming curr

ents.

c) The rain'

s releasing
finely-sensed

birthed-awak
ening

s.

d) (and after)

hushed almost
indecipher

able whisper
ings.

The persist

ent sound of
rain as the

wave's repeat
ed time-call

ings.

The Greeks

told these
storms just

right that
wrathed-in

tensity show
ering down.

Birds ex

ploring the
untold depth

of this sound
lessly grey-

sky.

Light

s across-the-
lake time-

sustaining
this myster

ious dark.

Mountain

s motionless
ly climbing

the weather
ed instinct

s of a time
less spell.

A moon

> less night
> ever-intent
>
> on its own
> indwelling
>
> silence
> s.

Ever

> greens climb
> ing the branch
>
> ed-length of
> their shadow
>
> ing still
> nesses.

A house

> of window
> s haunted
>
> with the e
> vil design
>
> s of its sol
> itary presen
>
> ce.

First morn

ing pleasure
boats water

ing the lake'
s easily com

pliant surfa
cing depth

s.

For Alena

at 13 if only
the changing

colors of
those precon

ceived dress-
designs could

fashion your
self out.

a) A reclusive

spider tenta
tively espy

ing the tense
stung-out

hold of its
poisonous

design
s.

b) Squashed-

hammered-
blood of its

sightless in
stantane

ous death-
down.

c) The summ

ing pianiss
imo of the

mosquito'
s space-

searching
blood-call

s.

d) The exact

ing hammer
ed scent of

a wood-pecker'
s worm-ripen

ed taste.

e) The illus

trious swan
upside-down

ed its white
ly immersing

hind–side
composure.

Board

walk's hamm
ered-down

wood's hollow
ing-out the

faintly-
felt sound

s of these
tentative

ly-held foot-
stepped call

ings.

Finely

meshed cur
tained–appear

ances mostly
dulled her

lonely sens
ed–for–be

ing.

a) The Autum

nal winds wild
ly invocating

a Derwish
danced the

supple tree
s in rhythm

ic response
loosed of

all their in
dwelling re

straint.

b) Is this

but a Bacchic
chant wined

to the vein
s of an in

stinctual
time–flow.

c) What's left

of the time
less Apollon

ic beauty
still–standing

its immovable
statuesque

accord
s.

d) blown from

the surety of
its dignified

source chaotic
ally soul–en

tranced.

e) Even the

soft-skinned
touch of the

lyre's lyrical
ly refined

sensibilit
ies hastened

to an abrupt
ly unwanton

close.

f) Birds no

longer grace
the heaven

s with the
silently un

folding wing
s of their

time–withhold
ing presence.

g) Whose command

ing voice can
be heard to

finally still
this all–con

suming chaos.

h) Or is it

but a sign of
the coming–

end a world be
reft of its

anchoring–
hold.

i) (and yet)

a sole unseen
bird voiced

to its irreg
ularly intun

ed song.

Mary Poppins

weather-um
brellaed to

a heavenly
time-color

ing expanse.

Isolated

stairs wind
ing-up through

the distance
s of sound

lessly ech
oings.

The winter

ed loneli
ness of Garda'

s bleakly a
bandoned

street
s.

These stone-

told reaches
of Garda's

time-emanci
pating cliff

s.

M. S.

that disease
initial

ed his name
now slowly

oncoming
caned to its

woodened rhy
thmically-up

holding pulse
d-stance.

And if

> there was noth
> ing more to
>
> be seen than
> the self-appar
>
> ent vacancy of
> eyes gazing
>
> intently
> back.

Only when

> the train sound
> lessly voiced
>
> moving through
> those interior
>
> landscape
> s of his.

A bird dis

> tantly sensed
> its voice
>
> still color
> lessly appar
>
> ent.

I sized-

him–up not as
a tailor with

his all–too–
familiar pin

s–and–needle
s to the

height of his
still unknown

response.

a) A young

girl with vague
ly surround

ing eyes must
have realized

that woman
hood's slow

ly becoming
the–more–of–

her.

b) A young

man's first–
felt needs

for an other
wise entic

ing complete
ness.

Fresh sea

breezes a
skin–sensed

touch of
self–desir

ing distanc
ings.

Why did

Adam realize
just then

that self–na
kedness.

The Jacob-

instinct bird–
nesting a home

less need for
a self–defin

ing domestic
tranquility.

Those Esau

s (even today)
animal-instinct

ing the blood-
scent of a

soulless
hunter.

Seemed (2)

a) After days

of suspend
ing rain the

clouds seem
ed astutely

self-confirm
ing.

b) That daily-

same slow-mov
ing passenger

boat seemed
my thought

s as well in
dwelling.

If that

first-seen'
s always–

now why wait
for anything

more.

A little

hesitant–
girl braid

ing her first–
seen steps

down their
feet-feel se

curing.

That night

with snow
piled-high

er than his
little dog'

s breadth-of-
seeing car

lights flash
ed his change-

of-sides
blood-esteem

ing death.

Realized

If you real

ize the extend
ed expanse of

her mother'
s matronly

establish
ment then

just imagine
what her

daughter'
s slimming

perspective
s might act

ually entail.

S. L.

argued for
Goethe's trans

parent simpli
cities where

as I counter
ed with Shake

speare's lin
guistic den

sity of depth
ed express

iveness.

Syncopations

Late autumn
al leaves

all-lined-
up for the

irregular
time-beat'

s falling-
off.

Beach-front

ed with the
facial façade

s of out–
framed

thought–emp
tiness

es.

Hand-in-

gloved presence
as if touch

could reveal
the ingrain

ed depth of
your feeling

s aloud.

A rest

less owner
as if his

hotel had
long been runn

ing away from
his unrequit

ed release.

She had

that fading
out–used look

of a woman
dreamless

ly forsaken.

Of exotic ori

gins she seem

ed somehow
out-of-place

as a rainy
tropical flow

er mutedly
ground-sensed.

Tommy final

ly slowing-
down aging

into a re
flective

ly quieting
uncertain

ty.

Open vista

s the lake
so intimate

ly perspect
ived even as

a fish pond
domestical

ly cultivat
ed.

A getting-

to-know-how
as eager dog

s sniffing-
out the for

eign scent
of strange

ly accommodat
ing habitat

s.

Scarsdalian

Those down-
town parades

fashioned
with the color

ful allure of
patriotic up

lifting flagg
ing after-

time communal-
eats.

He awoke in

the midst of
a dreamed-

intent author
lessly dia

logued.

Little girl

sliding-down
the inescap

able length
of her sens

ed time-
feel.

Psycholog

ically train
ed-to-listen

he disquieted
me with a dis

abled feel
ing of a list

ening-in-to-
telephone

call.

a) Where do

dreams come
from dialog

ing an unwritt
en script with

actors so fam
iliar (and

yet) intimate
ly otherwise.

b) Are dream

s an after-
time fulfill

ing of what
only could-

have-been.

c) Or are they

a mere flight-
of-fancying

a first-row
do-it-as-

it-seems pre
mière perform

ance.

d) He dream

ed far out to
the other-side

of a time-
witness

ing self.

e) Are those

don't-step-
beyond-fear

s of a death-
confining

uncertain
ty.

f) And of the

dead coming–
back to a

life of haunt
ed memorie

s.

g) Adolescent

wet–dream
s womaning

the beauty
of a bodi

less phant
om.

h) Turning

Aristotle
upside-down

time place
and person.

i) Are those

repetitive
dreams more

like a warn
ing-signal

don't touch
or ever step–

beyond.

j) Is Martin

Luther King's
"I have a

dream" (also)
what can't

be truly real
ized.

k) He dream

ed his thera
pist's suggest

ively receptive
know-how.

l) Dream-

world's fantas
y-finds those

veiled escap
ing hope-

route
s.

Something

of a felt-
softness in

the waves
this morning

caressing
her pillow'

s instinct
ive fantasie

s.

His prompt

ing smile im
personed

more of the
untouch

able depth
s of his va

cantly self–
enduring si

lence
s.

Sparrow'

s bread–speck
ed intens

ed–insist
ing taste–

find
s.

Jesus and the Angel *(Brescia)*

Jesus so
mildly suffer

ing as if
his flesh was

but melting–
alive for

love.

Sails hold

ing still
soundless

ly intact.

Testament

More–dead
than–alive

she gazed un
moved by her

own testimony
echoing–back

to haunt her
son's time–

precluding
childhood

love–length
s.

Only on the

last day did
the lake quiet–

down to the
resolving

stillness
of his own

length–of–
seeing.

Angelical

ly forming
clouds into

such sky-trans
parent imagin

ings.

A single

slightly
blood-stain

ed feather
in a remote

field of time-
remember

ing silence
s.

That tree

bushed-out
into leave

s so dense
ly self-in

habiting.

a) A life with

out love is
like a world

dulled in per
petual dark

ness.

b) As she her

self confided
lacking in

self–love
she could only

neighbor o
thers into much–

of–the–same.

c) Self-love

can dialogue

a self–inhab
iting loneli

ness.

d) or it can re

linguish its

own claims
for that of

another o
ver-coming

all-encompass
ing.

e) A mother'

s love though
self-sacrifi

cing should
never demand

an equival
ent response.

f) Adolescence

A mother'
s childhood

love may warm
th one's need

for a continu
ing beyond

one's newly
inhabited

self-presen
ce.

g) Love that

deaths its
always-being

a cold and
empty unin

habited
place.

h) Does death'

s loss-of–
love leave

one at the
self–love

start again.

i) or are those

years of self–

fulfilling
love continu

ing though
lesser–phrased

lighter-pulsed.

A fully

birded tree
may become

branched
in habit

ual song.

a) A window

less house
closed-in

to the shad
ows of self-

reflective
silence

s.

b) A world

without color
only the grey

and darkness
es of his

own self-con
fiding contem

plation
s.

c) Is there

here a no–
ways–out

all the door
s locked/barr

ed and the
keys time

lessly hidd
en.

d) Here are

the echoless
dead confin

ed to their
own self–shad

owing sound
less appear

ance
s.

e) Here are

their tomb–
stoned signa

tures the
only record

left of their
life's phantom

ed past.

f) The moon'

s whisper
ing silence

s as if the
dead could be

roused again
to the muted

light of their
timeless wan

dering
s.

"The Call" *(Gauguin)*

a) Can the

touched-light

coloring
s of but a

single self-re
fining flower

her hands a
gain just a mo

ment timeful
ly preserv

ed.

b) Or can the

darkening
prayers of a

self–enclos
ing Romanes

que church
realize The

Lord's speech
lessly awaken

ing presence.

c) That remem

bered night
when the dis

tant light of
those incom

ing wave
d into rhy

thmic flow
ing accord

s of our very-
being.

d) *If "a man*

and a woman
and a black

bird are one"
why fear its

darkly resound
ing wingèd-ap

praisal
s.

e) *Time and the*

river earth-
sourced the

boundless
confines of

the ocean's
tideful re

surgence
s.

f) *The night*

so vastly starr
ed its vivid

ly alert pre
sence.

g) When our

hands melt in
to the common

pulse of
timed–certain

ties.

Budded

flowers
tightly with

holding their
light–sensed

appearance
es.

Dark cloud

s resounding
a depth of o

minously
free–floating

foreboding
s.

a) The soft

light summer
rains touch

ing the skin'
s finely–

felt aware
nesses.

b) Autumnal

rains darken
ing the wind'

s intense
shadow

ings.

c) Winter

rains sensed
for the snow'

s purified a
wakening

s.

d) Spring

rains birth
ed in color

ed flower
ings.

Cactus

flowers pulsed
through

their dried–
spell's bright

nesses.

Rain drop

s running–
down their

windowed
perspect

ives.

Fossil

s re-timing
man's insist

ent urge for
depthed in

stinctual–
foreboding

s.

a) That lost

Malaysian
air flight

ed to the
bottomless

ocean's ti
dal sway

s.

b) The dead

off–course
from their

daily routine
as if time

doesn't con
tinually char

ter us to its
unknown where

about
s.

c) Not even a

clue of the
whys and

wheres as if
life and death'

s withholding
secrets could

become visual
ly certified.

Perhaps our

tragic Jewish
conscious

ness has dawn
ed the light

of a newly
birthed intrin

sically refin
ed fragile sen

sibility.

a) Saba'

s goat with
Jewish featur

ed into a
loneliness

of those
lost-tribe'

s wandering
s.

b) Saba's

"words" as a
means of es

cape into a
cleansed pur

ifying-re
birth.

c) Trieste

the city he
left behind

the last famil
iar quietude

of his Jew-
wandering

poetic-soul.

a) Leopardi'

s moon his
naked–woman

ed loved–
one's light o

pened eye
s to the

brighten
ed sadness

of veiled re
membranc

es.

b) Leopardi'

s infinity
envision

ed into
the depth

of a time
lessly re

called o
cean.

a) Pascoli'

s forsaken
nest symbol

of dream'
s recurrent

elusive per
suasion

s.

b) Pascoli'

s "cold summ
er of the

dead" November'
s barren empti

ness those
brittle fall

ing leave
s death–signa

tured.

a) Carducci'

s "Self–Portrait"
but a shadow

of himself a
framed picture

with only that
emptied frame

left intact.

b) The rhythm

ic spiritual
pulse of Car

ducci's bull'
s physical

ly enduring
patience

so Godly
formed.

Even the

great Michelan
gelo (Sonnet

285) let the
tools of his

divine inspir
ation rest

before the i
mage of Christ'

s cross–impell
ing sovereign

ty.

Can these

train-chang
ing landscape

my mind in
to those per

petually
uncertain

cloud-swell
s.

a) How does a

woman feel
an unseen life

dialogued
to the flesh

and blood of
her very-be

ing.

b) Are mother'

s rebirth
ed when life

emerges from
their only-

sourced self.

c) The death

of an unborn
baby is like

a budded flow
er darkly en

closed from
its light-im

pelling source.

a) Jackie

died at the
death of a

single mo
ment as a

candle touch
ed-out of

its indwell
ing light.

b) His funeral

witnessing
the time-

length per
spective

s of a multi-
personed

being.

c) They'll all

die at once
as if that

death-mo
ment had be

come sourced
in a perpet

ual now.

a) Can a liv

ing faith die
from its daily

used-out pre
sence.

b) Or is faith

a self-renew
ing source

as Moses' time
less witness

ing of the
burning bush.

That late

August feel
ing of the

slowly increa
sing summ

er's outlast
ing decline.

Italian

romantic
poetry so

oft attuned
to the long

ing sadness
of an irretrie

vable loss.

a) Do nation

s also die
and become re

birthed in a
cycle of con

tinuing change.

b) Or is the

life-span of
history a

guided phas
ing to its

self-fulfill
ing close.

c) Still life

s as a dis
tantly inspok

en landscap
ing a sense

of perpetual
ly pre-design

ed permanen
ce.

d) Is poetry

the swan-song
of life's

vanishing
beautie

s.

For Rosemarie

Why is first
love so poet

ically cher
ished how

ever fresh it
may seem when

its flame may
die a slow

ly self-con
suming death

whereas last
ing love e

ven when lower-
flamed become

s time
lessly sourc

ed.

a) They live

the life of
death–breed

ing tunnel
s shadowy

underground
persons as

rats gnawing
at the very–

roots of life'
s renewing sub

stance.

b) Killing if

only women and
children opport

uned their a
rousing daily–

commerse.

c) The moon e

ven its dimin
ishing light

raised their
tidal lust–

urging
s.

d) They daily

relished in
the blood of

death's sup
reme calling

s.

e) The good

and the beauti
ful but idol

s of their
hate-entrall

ing faith.

f) Death had

become their
martyrer's

wanton end
flagged in

the pitch-
darkness

of self-con
cealing under

ground person
less being

s.

g) Had Satan

become master
of their life-

impulsing
death-instin

cts.

h) How even

each common
ly colored

untouched
flower be

comes but a
symbol of

life's self-
enduring con

tinuity.

i) And Israel

God's chosen
but a pawn

in man's fate
ful search

even for a
tainted sur

vival.

a) Petrarch'

s love poem
s possess

ed of such
an obsess

ive sameness
as if unful

filled love
could ever

lose its all–
encompass

ing hold–on–
us.

b) Always eyes

and hair Amor'
s incessant love–

darts piercing
ever-deeper

than time
could possib

ly endure.

c) Laura

had become so
much an ideal

eternally
conceived as

a statue that
even if flesh

ed and blood
ed never real

ly true-to-
life.

d) Had Petrarch'

s love of love-
for-its-own-

sake cast a
spell even u

pon Laura's
own genuine

credibil
ity.

e) For those a

ging-in-love
Petrarch

may also be
read as an

almost adol
escent unre

solving obsess
ion.

This oncom

ing night in
creasing

the depthed-
darkness of

these wood'
s shadowing

presence.

Lights sig

nalling a dis
tant silent

source awaken
ing an imag

inary time-
sense.

Our train

mysterious
ly live to

the moon'
s impending

silence
s.

Night

clouds reach
ing even bey

ond the hori
zon's indwell

ing darkness
es.

a) The Lord'

s holiness
may not prove

as humane as
we would

(perhaps)
like-it-to-

be.

b) Guilt

(as with King
David) hurts

the most when
it's bled-o

pen into the
mainstream

s of one's
very-being.

c) Cutting-off

what the bible
insists on

telling us
has become a

modern way of
creating God

in our own–
wishful-i

mage.

d) Even a bad

conscience
can be dull

ed-down (as
with King David)

when desire o
verwhelm

s The Lord'
s own command

ing right
eousness.

e) King David'

s passionate
nature (as

with St. Paul)
can equally re

veal-in-sin
as in their

self reclaim
ing need for

God's eternal
righteous

ness.

f) Was the na

kedly-bathing-
Bathseba (cer

tainly within
range of David'

s alluring
eyes) complete

ly innocent
of their fut

ure cohabitat
ion.

g) David's sad

istic play with
his faithful

"servant"
Uria reveal

ing the depth
of evil-design

s within this
so-called

"just king".

h) God's judg

ment on Bath
seba's prag

nant child and
on David's

heirs leave
little consol

ation left for
a death-living

king.

i) (and yet)

David's ulti
mate heir

the "king of
kings" right

ing David's (and
our own) sinful

ly-depthed
endeavor

s.

Success story *(the American Dream) (5)*

a) *"Rags-to-*

riches" (the

American
dream) may beg-

the-question
of a blemish

ed (no-hold
s-barred)

means of a
certained

ascent.

b) *Good work*

s (however mor
ally justif

ied) may soothe
one's uneas

ing self-re
assuring

conscience.

c) Pink's up

staired self-
satisfying

down-looking
on those

night-mared
fears of a

bottomless
pit.

d) He closely

suited himself
into the

self-mirror
ing pleasure

s of a tweed-
style comfort

ability.

e) "Nothing

succeeds like
(the) success"

of reaching
that timeless

ly-evading
peak of self-

ascending pro
minence.

a) When one

movement
leads to

continu
ing time-e

lusive shad
owing

s.

b) Pink at the

height of
his self-suited–

smile estab
lishing a

ready pose
for his

emanating pre-
assurance

s.

c) Poems

leave be
hind their

own indeli
ble time–

imprint.

d) At the bal

conie's sky-
immersing

those inter
ior space

s of vast
ly horizon

ed sensibil
ities.

e) Today as

any day's
intricate

success
ion of spid

er-webbed
transpar

encie
s.

The scent

of autumn
as stone

flower
s breath

ing the
light of time

less distanc
ings.

Hammershøi

a quiet
almost imper

sonal sense
of interior

contemplat
ion permeate

s Hammershoi'
s atmospher

ic self-en
closing still

nesses.

Eisenstadt *(Haydn Festival)*

Train's light
s restless

ly sounding
the field's

indwelling
composure

s.

Her eyes

bulged reson
ating thought–

claims.

Pink'

> s cushion
> ed feeling-
>
> at-home com
> fort restful
>
> ly self-satis
> fying.

Old-fashion

> ed wooden
> bridge expand
>
> ing the space
> ful length of
>
> its timed con
> templation
>
> s.

Frolic

> ing spring-
> like flower
>
> s train-track
> ed to speed
>
> ful undeterr
> ing distanc
>
> ings.

For Rosemarie

A touched-
look center

ed those un
spoken silen

ces of our
s.

Why do

those empty
train-station

ed seats seem
so time-promp

ting.

Leaves fall

ing through
their time

lessly color
ed remembran

ces.

The train

stopped in
to the cur

tained–length
of its still–

standing win
dowed–presen

ce.

A subdued

sense of light
atmospher

ed this late
summer day in

to Corot–like
impression

ed transpar
encies.

Haydn's 98th *(last mvt)*

single–them
ed us into

the starts
and stops of

catch–me–if–
you–never–

can finality
of unerring

butterfly–
chasing

s.

Mozart's

C Minor Piano
Concerto

double–dia
logued recurr

ing self–shad
owings lyri

cally attun
ing life's

powerful
ly dramatic–

insistence.

98th *Symphony* (trio)

Haydn's pea
sant dance

s sun-shine
me into Breugh

el-like timed-
impulsing

s.

If life'

s more than
art why not

simply live-
it-out until

it lives-
you-down to

its bare-
thread final

ities.

Had Mozart

and his art
become a

unity sourced
in elusive

ly depthed
rhythmic

current
s.

a) Do we need

a nostalgic
distance

from person
and place

(Verga) to
realize their

(and our)
most intimate

ly personal-
being.

b) Or does the

now and ever-
present dia

logue us in
to such a

depthed-under
standing.

These time-

intending
hills flow

ing us in
to their pre-

destined un
certaint

ies.

Sopron (Hungary) (5)

a) Over the bor

der of time
and place a

world apart
strangely

tongued for
eign even to

the common
usage of sound

and sense.

b) A goat-dedi

cated church
emblemati

cally horned
with a remote

ly indistinct
Christian

dialect.

c) The fire

towering
over a city

burnt with
the fuelling

rage of its
war-time endem

ic fear
s.

d) a small

Jewish commun
ity huddled

in the bare-
bred shadow

s of its time-
enduring chos

enness.

e) After the

holocaust

only a few
Jews left

to a tiny
medieval

Gothic syn
agogue and a

purifying
bath depthed

deeply beyond
reach of its

satanical pur
suers.

A clear-

blue day as
the clarify

ing purity
of a sun–

breathed
Haydn quartet.

Rows of cere

monial-like
pidgeons

peopling
their early

morning roof
ed sit-down

contemplat
ions.

Schubert'

s thunderous
"Quartet Move

ment"'s con
tinuous re

miniscence
of times that

have remain
ed unsaid-in-

passing.

a) Mozart's

"Dissonant
Quartet'"

s slow intro
duction Haydn–

like world
depthed in

time–withhold
ing contempla

tions.

b) the slow

movement's most
especially

intimately-
personal re

petitive
phrasing

s.

Haydn Quartet Op. 33,3

Can one title
a hymnally-

spaced relig
iously indwell

ing movement
times ahead

of itself
"scherzo".

a) When the

sun has turn
ed-the-cor

ner on a
late summer

afternoon
and left cool

ly shadowed
impression

s of person'
s still faint

ly light-in
habiting.

b) Pave stone'

s soundless
ly measur

ing these
foot-timed

echoing-per
spective

s.

c) Does the fa

cial image of
one long–

dead tempor
arily revive

a moment of
his life–be

ing.

d) Shopping

window's
glass façade

s reflect
ing a fleet

ing impress
ion of a wo

man's instin
ctive buy (by)–

passing
s.

Feeling-

out the in
creasing

height of a
contempor

ary tree
left Pink

climbing
his inadept

ly equipped
imagination.

Slow Movement *(Abel op. 6,5, Flute Concerto)*

as if the
scene had chang

ed into a
world of in

tuitively-
touched sad

ly-felt re
flection

s.

Mozart Violin Concerto 4 *(finale)*

a catchy
touch-me-no

finds fin
ale.

Haydn's

Symphonies 33
and 72'

s question-
and-answer

dialogue
lyrical

ly time-re
solving.

Dark win

dows closing-
down secret

ly withhold
ing passage

s of the
mind-sense.

Our hotel

carpet's
diffuse

ly coloring
elusive

ly extend
ing time-en

closing e
choing

s.

After

taste of that
small Hungar

ian city
left me with

a strange
ly uncertain

ed feeling
of Jews not-

so-readily
bought-free.

Pleyel Trio *(Sonata Ben 434)*

One can't i
mitate Haydn'

s efferves
cent instinct

ual otherwise
ness.

Haydn Trio 16

slow movement
somehow world

s apart evas
ively unfami

liar.

Mozart Rondo

in A Minor
reveries

of sound-
touched mo

ments ines
capably

cloud-trans
forming.

Early morn

ing light-per
suasion

s the minor
tonalitie

s of over
coming Mozart

ean poetic-
sadness

es.

Leopardi'

    s early 19th
    century e

    legies for
    the-once-that-

    was-Italy
    knows no be

    ginning nor
    end only the

    devastation
    of the here-

    now mourning
    blood-spill

    ed distant
    from its holy

    soil need
    less but for

    foreign gain.

That tree-

    bound lonely
    bird-song re

    mains the e
    choing image

    of Leopardi'
    s time-wing

    èd verse
    s.

When there'

s nothing
left-to-do

but to seek-
out time'

s space
less phras

ings.

Kraus

Violin Concerto

not for beauty
or the instru

ment's sake
(however de

manding)
but as a

fine Haydn
symphony

evolving a
thought–

sound time-
securing

form–assur
ance.

Haffner

Symphony (Mo
zart) instru

mentally
festive pro

vocative
sound–color

ings.

Haydn "Clock

Symphony no. 101"

the slow intro
duction a cur

tain–raising
cosmic view

of timed–spa
cial sound–

intensitie
s.

As if dance

had become the
perennial

source of
sound–awared

rhythmic–
impulsing

s.

a) If poetry

should reclaim
the idyllic

purity of
pastoral pleas

ures (Croce)
our modern

times remain
poetical

ly dulled–
down defici

ently insen
sitive.

b) Only the

cleansed-re
newal of the

lingustical
ly acute voice

can assure
the rock-bott

om basis of a
genuinely

refined poet
ic revival.

c) In the be

ginning the
word's God-

given indig
enously

creative
source.

The lone pidg

    eon isolated

    on that in
    dwelling

    roof had be
    come but a

    still-life
    inadequate

    ly self-en
    dowed.

Early morn

    ing work ef
    ficiency

    may become
    papered to

    the mine-bod
    ie's untouch

    ably elusive
    self-redeem

    ing need
    s.

Fly poised

on opposite
side of the

window design
ing finely

finger–im
pressed wait

ings for its
wingèd time–

releasing
s.

Whitely–

meshed cur
tains self–

protecting
her sensed–

bodied reap
raisal

s.

Do such

tiny–toy dog
s endow their

sovereign
masters with a

higher–proport
ioned sense

of predomin
antly expos

ing self–im
portance.

Esterházy'

s self–impos
ing castle

d me into
its window–

rowed glass
ed–imaginat

ions.

He sat an

excitable
look–down

sit–postur
ed insatia

ble impuls
ings.

He "walked"

like an arti
ficially

zooed-animal
pawed forward

feet-encircl
ing a round

phrasing
s.

Last Jew

left in Eisen
stadt ghett

oed to pre-
holocaust

fear-arous
ings.

Slight

ly blue-white
cloud-view

innocent
ly child-like

dream-awaken
ings.

a) Trio 25

à la Hongroise

(slow mvt.)

Haydn's soft
ly tender

blossoming
middle–aged

love–call
s.

b) À la Hong

roise exotical
ly–gypsy fire–

side rhythmic
ally dance–

enflamed.

Mischa Maisky'

s impassion
ed cello–ac

cords as rich
ly colored

as Brahms'
op. 8 trio.

a) Brahms' op. 8

trio (slow

movement)

immensed a
spacious

depth time
lessly self–

impending.

b) That horse-

trot scherzo
Beethovian

dance–impress
ioned hear–

says.

c) The passion

ate outer–
movement

s so dense
ly darken

ed labyrin
thed self–

enclosure
s.

D. P. Newspapers

mid–1945
death-number

ed displaced
persons paper

ed their way
back to a

long-lost
half-forgott

en biblical
ly indwell

ing home-
land.

a) Has it be

come an allus
ive aspect

of woman's
most intri

cate nature
to color–

dress their
intimate

ly instinct
ual self-re

vealing de
sires.

b) Do young

girls prettify
their hand–

down puppet
s in their

own careful
ly assessed

self–imaged
imaginat

ion.

Sky-grey

morning left
those circl

ing bird
s distant

ly called
from a truly

self–encompass
ing home–

sense.

Eisenstadt Sept. 11 *(5)*

a) Mozart Symph

ony 20

Early Mozart
symphonie

s oft more
felt than

found-out a
contrast

ing of un
equalled

sound-depth
s.

b) Kraft Cello

Sonata 4

composed
more for the

cello's self-
sake virtuo

so display
ing even

(at time
s) lyri

cally conceiv
ed after

thought
s.

c) How could

musicologi
ists ever

have attri
buted Haydn'

s self-confin
ing lyrical

loveliness
to their im

itative play–
it-all-off

Kraftful.

d) Haydn'

s "Miracle"
Symphony 96

more a mir
acle of in

novative
let's-get-it-

all-right be
fore it get

s us down-
sighted.

e) Another

Abel mostly
unknown slow

movement of
an almost

hymnal grace
fullness.

For Warren (2)

a) Can quest

ions become
more self-en

circling bird-
wise than an

swered for
landing–

right
s.

b) À la Petrarch

Can a master
of form and

language
counter a

sameness
of pre-real

izing express
iveness.

A pyramid

> of pigeon
> s roof-sitt
>
> ing a collect
> ive unity of
>
> cloud conform
> ing sit-down
> s.

Wind-whisper

> ing rain-touch
> ed silence
>
> s a hushed
> never-but–
>
> now.

Windowed

> time-reflect
> ing all of
>
> her emptied-
> room loneli
>
> nesses.

Indwelling

intertwin
ing passage

s of a laby
rinthed

no-ways-out.

Pink

after reali
zing that e

ven "birds-
of-a-feather"

ed change
able color

ings suited
his own pri

vately aspir
ing taste

as well.

Ugly paint

ings wall-
hanging your

insufficient
ly posing

hands–in–deed'
s pocket

ing.

Chinese

fish silver
ed the touch

ed–silence
s of moon–

lit perspect
ives.

a) Bilingual

Transform
ed into a

radiant
woman low–

pitched pre-
tuned through

manly–intent
phrasing

s.

b) He-she

"married"
to a two-

selved im
personed

store-shop
life-appar

ent manne
quin.

c) He chang

ed his God-in
tending per

son into an
enigmatic

replica of
a most woman

ly recepti
vity.

d) Aren't we

all (though)

representa
tional piece

s piano-placed
for Chopin

esque melodic
moon-lit

smiling
s.

She dress

ed so neat
ly fit that

cleansed
look of her

shadowless
presence.

For Rosemarie

The soft

sway of wave
s danced

her into
that faint

ly rhythm
mic pulse of

time-color
ings.

Could it e

ver become
darker (self-

enclosing)
than not e

ven sensing
the where of

possibly see
ing through.

a) They won

first prize
for restor

ing the tru
ly histori

cal mediev
al confine

s of an empt
ied-out soul

less Jewish
synagogue.

b) Only the

names and
dates of the

war-timed de
ported neat

ly listed
row upon row

on a wall
ed vacant

ness.

Are we all

Achilles-heel
ed at that

bottom-length
of our own

time-reach.

For Rosemarie *(53rd Anniversary)*

> Time has heal
> ed my dark
>
> ly conceal
> ed wound
>
> s through
> the soft
>
> ness of your
> indwelling
>
> warmth–embra
> cings.

If we could

> envision that
> all–of–a–sin
>
> gle–moment
> would cer
>
> tain a complete
> ness of our
>
> own selved–
> being?

Is dawn

> that oncom
> ing birth of
>
> a light–in
> dwelling
>
> awareness.

Flash-back

moments in
stinctive

ly alive to
those darkly

secret unin
habited silen

ces.

After Thorstein Veblen *(for Erich)*

The wood-

work finish
of a fresh

ly complet
ed balcony

lengthed
and confined

to his self–
satisfying

presence.

She stanced

    like a cat
ready to

    spring-out
paws first

    blood-insight
ing.

In the poet'

    s birthday
room 6am

    as a little
girl wonder

    ing where to
find that mag

    ic wand of
his.

He mirror

    ed his own i
mage on

    those who
kept looking

    back.

Saying just

    the right
things in a

    pre-determin
ed way often

    wrongs your
own untouch

    able sense of
each inescap

    able moment.

Those silent

    to evil speak
louder than

    words could
possibly an

    swer.

These rain

    ed-down silen
ces scarce

    ly sensed
time-spell

    ed.

Early autumn'

s as transit
ionally color

ed as the
mood-swing

s of adoles
cent sensibili

ties.

a) Lermontov'

s demonical
ly-angelic

darkness
es the poet

ic urge of
a life-or-

nothing sur
vival instin

ct.

b) Lermontov'

s passion
ate self-duell

ing instinct
s blooded his

last poetic
ally time-en

during phras
ings.

c) The Cauca

sus landscap
ed his primi

evally mount
ainous self-en

during instin
ctual climb

s.

Nineveh 2013

Over-ripen
ed fruit Nahum-

like dropping
its last

time-sourced
prophetic

offering
s.

What Jesus

left unspoken
(as Israel'

s prophetic
future)

speaks for
itself time

lessly self–
perpetuat

ing.

Over-green

ed leaves their
yellowing

saturated
death–impress

ed foreboding
s.

DP's *(displaced persons) (7)*

a) Those who

stayed after

the war's last
ing hate in

their heart'
s life-

blood paled
to a displac

ed time-rhy
thm.

b) Those who

lived through
it all as if

death had
been lowered

from its
feared and

foreign pre
sence to but

the banality
of a daily

routine.

c) Those who

stayed on
with a liv

ing guilt
shadowing

the depth
s of their

daily pre
sence.

d) Their child

ren born to
be cut-off

from their
parent's

time-indwell
ing blood–

stream.

e) A new life

in Israel or
America as

if life could
be redeemed

from the liv
ing shadow

s of an un
known past.

f) The wander

ing tribes
of Israel

homed to the
living fear

of a new-
wheres-else

"final solut
ion".

g) Their preda

tors newly a
wakening

the desert
lands to a

time-impend
ing blood-

thirst.

"His blood

come over us
and our child

ren" Is Jesus
blood only

that of "an
eye for an

eye" or more
so the ever

lasting bond
of His redeem

ing compass
ion.

When the cur

tain to the
holy of hol

ies split
right-down

the middle
was that a

spiritual
circumcis

ion to His
life-compell

ing being.

For S. L.

Does listen
ing to the

same music
your way

or mine
transform

what's act
ually heard.

"Reborn"

Does His love
(or even

ours) re
create the

wordless
pulse of our

very-being.

Autumn

al birds pre
paring for

their instin
ctual flight

distancing
even beyond

the mountain'
s irresist

ible scope.

Is there

a residue
called "self"

at the blood-
bottom of our

ever-shift
ing tidal-im

pulsing
s.

Touching

the moon'
s surface

isn't the
same as real

izing its
light-eman

ating sourc
ed-being.

Myths and

dreams allur
ing a world

darkly inhab
ited time-

shifting.

The white-

shine of
your naked

body's moon-
intensing

glow.

The thorn

ed touch of

blackberry
blood inti

mately pain
ed.

Out of the

mist the morn
ing arising

its self-im
pending

call.

Poetry books by David Jaffin

1. **Conformed to Stone,** Abelard-Schuman, New York 1968, London 1970.

2. **Emptied Spaces,** with an illustration by Jacques Lipschitz, Abelard-Schuman, London 1972.

3. **In the Glass of Winter,** Abelard-Schuman, London 1975, with an illustration by Mordechai Ardon.

4. **As One,** The Elizabeth Press, New Rochelle, N. Y. 1975.

5. **The Half of a Circle,** The Elizabeth Press, New Rochelle, N. Y. 1977.

6. **Space of,** The Elizabeth Press, New Rochelle, N. Y. 1978.

7. **Preceptions,** The Elizabeth Press, New Rochelle, N. Y. 1979.

8. **For the Finger's Want of Sound,** Shearsman Plymouth, England 1982.

9. **The Density for Color,** Shearsman Plymouth, England 1982.

10. **Selected Poems** with an illustration by Mordechai Ardon, English/Hebrew, Massada Publishers, Givatyim, Israel 1982.

11. **The Telling of Time,** Shearsman Books, Kentisbeare, England 2000 and Johannis, Lahr, Germany.

12. **That Sense for Meaning,** Shearsman Books, Kentisbeare, England 2001 and Johannis, Lahr, Germany.

13. **Into the timeless Deep,** Shearsman Books, Kentisbeare, England 2003 and Johannis, Lahr, Germany.

14. **A Birth in Seeing,** Shearsman Books, Exeter, England 2003 and Johannis, Lahr, Germany.

15. **Through Lost Silences,** Shearsman Books, Exeter, England 2003 and Johannis, Lahr, Germany.

16. **A voiced Awakening,** Shearsman Books, Exter, England 2004 and Johannis, Lahr, Germany.

17. **These Time–Shifting Thoughts**, Shearsman Books, Exeter, England 2005 and Johannis, Lahr, Germany.

18. **Intimacies of Sound,** Shearsman Books, Exeter, England 2005 and Johannis, Lahr, Germany.

19. **Dream Flow** with an illustration by Charles Seliger, Shearsman Books, Exeter, England 2006 and Johannis, Lahr, Germany.

20. **Sunstreams** with an illustration by Charles Seliger, Shearsman Books, Exeter, England 2007 and Johannis, Lahr, Germany.

21. **Thought Colors,** with an illustration by Charles Seliger, Shearsman Books, Exeter, England 2008 and Johannis, Lahr, Germany.

22. **Eye-Sensing,** Ahadada, Tokyo, Japan and Toronto, Canada 2008.

23. **Wind-phrasings,** with an illustration by Charles Seliger, Shearsman Books, Exeter, England 2009 and Johannis, Lahr, Germany.

24. **Time shadows,** with an illustration by Charles Seliger, Shearsman Books, Exeter, England 2009 and Johannis, Lahr, Germany.

25. **A World mapped-out,** with an illustration by Charles Seliger, Shearsman Books, Exeter, England 2010.

26. **Light Paths,** with an illustration by Charles Seliger, Shearsman Books, Exeter, England 2011 and Edition Wortschatz, Schwarzenfeld, Germany.

27. **Always Now,** with an illustration by Charles Seliger, Shearsman Books, Bristol, England 2012 and Edition Wortschatz, Schwarzenfeld, Germany.

28. **Labyrinthed,** with an illustration by Charles Seliger, Shearsman Books, Bristol, England 2012 and Edition Wortschatz, Schwarzenfeld, Germany.

29. **The Other Side of Self,** with an illustration by Charles Seliger, Shearsman Books, Bristol, England 2012 and Edition Wortschatz, Schwarzenfeld, Germany.

30. **Light Sources,** with an illustration by Charles Seliger, Shearsman Books, Bristol, England 2013 and Edition Wortschatz, Schwarzenfeld, Germany.

31. **Landing Rights,** with an illustration by Charles Seliger, Shearsman Books, Bristol, England 2014 and Edition Wortschatz, Schwarzenfeld, Germany.

32. **Listening to Silence,** with an illustration by Charles Seliger, Shearsman Books, Bristol, England 2014 and Edition Wortschatz, Schwarzenfeld, Germany.

33. **Taking Leave,** with an illustration by Mei Fêng, Shearsman Books, Bristol, England 2014 and Edition Wortschatz, Schwarzenfeld, Germany.

34. **Jewel Sensed,** with an illustration by Paul Klee, Shearsman Books, Bristol, England 2015 and Edition Wortschatz, Schwarzenfeld, Germany.

35. **Shadowing Images**, with an illustration by Pieter de Hooch, Shearsman Books, Bristol, England 2015 and Edition Wortschatz, Schwarzenfeld.

36. **Untouched Silences**, with an illustration
by Paul Seehaus, Shearsman Books, Bristol,
England 2016 and Edition Wortschatz,
Schwarzenfeld.

37. **Soundlesss Impressions**, with an illustration
by Qi Baishi, Shearsman Books, Bristol,
England 2016 and Edition Wortschatz,
Schwarzenfeld.

38. **Moon Flowers**, with a photograph by
Hannelore Bäumler, Shearsman Books,
Bristol, England 2017 and Edition Wortschatz,
Schwarzenfeld.

Book on David Jaffin's poetry: Warren Fulton,
Poemed on a beach, Ahadada, Tokyo, Japan
and Toronto, Canada 2010.